# THE ISLAND OF
# MAUI

# MAUI NŌ KA ʻOI
## Maui is indeed the best

**BONECHI**

# HAWAII CALLS, INC.

d.b.a. Ahi Paka, Travel-Lite, Hula Records, Kona-Kai Distributing Co.
99-139 Waiua Way, Unit #56. ʻAiea, HI 96701-3288
Ph: (808) 485-2294/(800) 756-4852   Fx (808) 485-2296/(800) 316-3547
Website: www.hawaiicalls.com      E-mail: hularecords@hawaii.rr.com

# INDEX

## Pronunciation of Hawaiian

Consonants:

**p, k**  about as in English but with less aspiration.
**h, l, m, n**  about as in English; *l* may be dental-alveolar and *n* dental.
**w**  after *i* and *e* usually a lax *v*; after *u* and *o* usually like *w*; after *a* or initially, like *w* or *v*.
**ʻ**  a glottal stop, similar to the sound between the *oh's* in English *oh-oh*.

Vowels:

*Unstressed*

| | | |
|---|---|---|
| a | like *a* in above | |
| e | like *e* in bet | |
| i | like *y* in city | |
| o | like *o* in sole | } but without off-glides |
| u | like *oo* in moon | |

*Stressed*

| | | |
|---|---|---|
| a, ā | like *a* in far | } |
| e | like *e* in bet | but without off-glides; vowels |
| ē | like *ay* in pay | marked with macrons are |
| i, ī | like *ee* in see | somewhat longer than other |
| o, ō | like *o* in sole | vowels and are always stressed |
| u, ū | like *oo* in moon | |

For additional helpful information about the Hawaiian language, readers should consult the New Pocket Hawaiian Dictionary, by Mary Kawena Pukui and Samuel H. Elbert, University of Hawaii Press.

*Project:* Casa Editrice Bonechi
*Editorial Director:* Monica Bonechi
*Picture Research and Graphic Design:* Monica Bonechi
*Video Page Making and Cover:* Manuela Ranfagni
*Editing:* Rita Bianucci

*Texts:* Leonardo Olmi
*Captions and revision:* Rita Bianucci
*Translation:* Julia Weiss Goldin

*The photographs contained in this volume are by* Leonardo Olmi

*For the revision of the Hawaiian terms we thank*
Fred Kalani Meinecke, Assistant Professor, Hawaiian Language, University of Hawaiʻi, Windward Community College

© Copyright by Casa Editrice Bonechi - Florence, Italy
Ph.: +39 055 576841 - Fax: +39 055 5000766
E-mail: bonechi@bonechi.it - Internet: www.bonechi.it

*Printed in Italy by* Centro Stampa Editoriale Bonechi

**ISBN 88-476-0773-6**

* * *

# INTRODUCTION

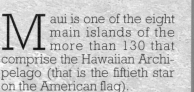

Maui is one of the eight main islands of the more than 130 that comprise the Hawaiian Archipelago (that is the fiftieth star on the American flag).
*Maui nō ka ʻoi*, as it is commonly called in the local language, means "Maui is the best". Maui is the second largest of the Hawaiian islands and a favorite vacation destination for travelers from the world over. Every year, beautiful beaches with crystal clear waters, migrating whales, fantastic golf courses, green mountains covered with lush rain forests, spectacular waterfalls, frequent and brilliantly hued rainbows, an enormous volcano that resembles a moonscape and gigantic waves that make it the world's surfing capital draw millions of tourists.

When you arrive at the airport a colorful, fragrant garland, known as a *lei* will be put around your neck as you hear "Aloha", the traditional word of welcome. At this point you are officially in Hawaiʻi, a favourite destination for tourists from all over the world. The beaches are golden, the cobalt blue of the ocean blends with the outlines of the nearby islands on the horizon, a gentle breeze picks up the waves that are ridden by the colored sails of the windsurfers, and behind us the green mountains of the west coast soar towards the blue sky. It is the truth: *Maui nō ka ʻoi* is precisely what Capitan Cook might have thought when he reached Hawaiʻi from Polynesia in 1778 as he searched for a sea link between the Pacific and Atlantic Oceans.

The island may owe much to the demigod Māui (from which it gets its name). According to an ancient Polynesian legend, Māui could not bear to have the Sun shine on the island (where he lived) for just a few hours a day so that the women could not dry their clothes or prepare food while it was still daylight. Infuriated, he decided to climb to the top of the Haleakalā volcano to capture the sun's rays with a rope of coconut fibers. When Māui threatened to kill him, the Sun begged for mercy and promised to cross the island more slowly. If we want to believe this legend, we must admit that the demigod Māui certainly achieved what he wanted!

In 1790 the famous king Kamehameha the Great, came from the Big Island and landed on the southeastern coast of Maui with his warriors. He headed from Hāna towards Wailuku where, during a bloody battle beneath the ʻIao Needle he defeated the warriors of Kalanikūpule, son of the king of Maui.

After the defeat, prince Kalanikūpule fled to the island of Oʻahu where Kamehameha defeated him definitively in the battle of Nuʻuanu Pali. Thus, King Kamehameha succeeded in unifying the Hawaiian islands. After the death of Kamehameha the Great, his successor Kamehameha II was so fascinated by the tropical beauty of Maui that in 1820 he elected Lahaina as the capital of his kingdom. The city of Lahaina was the seat of the Hawaiian government until 1845 when the capital was moved to Honolulu.

# WHALES

**L**ahaina and Ma'alaea are the main ports of departure for whale-watching boats.

One of the main organizations engaged in this activity is the Pacific Whale Foundation, a not-for-profit association that uses the money it earns to protect the *Megaptera novaeangliae*, that is, the humpback whales of the Pacific from extinction. The foundation studies the behavior of these whales and tries to educate the public about these cetaceans and to teach respect and conservation of the marine environment. It has been estimated that 3,000 to 4,000 humpback whales of the North Pacific spend the summer in the cold waters off the Alaskan coast to then migrate – from November to May – to the warm waters of Maui. This is their ideal home where, relatively far from predators they can mate, give birth and raise their young.

*Boats take tourists out for a close-up viewing of the humpback whales: watching them breach is an unforgettable experience.*

KAULANA

These whales can grow to a maximum length of 50 feet (15 meters), they love shallow waters and for this reason they selected the ʻAuʻau Channel between Maui and Lānaʻi where the water is no more than about 300 feet (100 meters) deep. From December to May (even though February is considered the best month of all) the Pacific Whale Foundation's boats guarantee a meeting with these magnificent creatures.

Sometimes, just a few yards from the boat they will show you their humps and tails, wave a greeting with their pectoral fins or on a lucky day, they will jump out of the water – that is known as breaching. The experience becomes even more interesting when a hydrophone is put in the water and connected to amplifiers so that you can even hear them sing.

*Humpback whales are skilled acrobats. No longer hunted, these huge and harmless cetaceans stay in the hospitable waters of Hawaiʻi from November through May during the calving season. On the following pages, a humpback during a spectacular breach.*

# HANG LOOSE

Hang loose is a gesture typical to Maui. People make a fist with the right hand, and with thumb and pinky raised rotate it as they say "*Aloha*." The proper response is a similar gesture, but it does take some practice to do it right. The words for "thank-you" are **mahalo**, or **mahalo nui loa**, thanks a million!

*Standing next to a gaily painted 'fifties Mercury, a man gives the traditional Hawaiian greeting. An islander, dressed in the traditional way, with a crown of lei, makes the same sign.*

# HULA and LŪ'AU

Many of the big hotels on the northwestern side of Maui such as the Marriott offer *lū'au*, the traditional Hawaiian outdoor feast. The main dish is pork baked in an *imu,* that is, an underground oven. The evening is enlivened by Hawaiian music and beautiful *hula* dancers adorned with garlands, *leis*. The Hula is a sacred dance inspired by nature, like the leaves swaying in the wind and the slow, sensual movements of the waves as they roll onto the sand. The music has a charm all its own: the distinctive melodies are played on instruments such as the *kālā'au* (rhythm sticks), *'ukulele*, steel guitar, *pū'ili* (bamboo wands) and sharkskin drums.

*Music and dances that are of sacred origin enliven the sweet nights in the Hawaiian islands. The costumes, ornaments and tattoos that adorn the dancers bodies in a triumph of color are Polynesian, as were the first people who settled in Hawai'i.*

# LAHAINA

Lahaina is the largest business center on Maui as well as the island's liveliest and most famous resort. Starting in 1819 for over forty years it was one of the world's major whaling ports. Lahaina offered a safe harbor under all weather conditions, so up to fifty whaling ships could be anchored there at once. Pacific whale hunting began to decline around 1860, but even though more than a century has passed, we can still feel the atmosphere of those years thanks to the well-restored typical wooden homes, the photographs and whalers' mementoes that are displayed in many spots. Therefore, a visit to the **Carthaginian II Floating Museum** is a must. It is a square-rigged ship anchored in the port of Lahaina, a faithful replica of the Carthaginian I that sank in 1972. Inside the museum we can see weapons used for whale hunting and a exhibit entitled "The

*The port of Lahaina with the West Maui Mountains in the background.*

World of the Whale" that explains many interesting aspects of the humpback whales' lives.

Taking a walk along **Front Street** along the shore we will come to the **Richards House**, the first building in the islands to be built entirely of coral blocks. It was the home of William Richards, the first protestant missionary to reach Lahaina, who was King Kamehameha III's tutor and translator. The **Hale Pa'ahao**, which means "prison" in Hawaiian is one of the oldest buildings in Lahaina, dating from 1850. It was used to imprison those guilty of crimes such as mutiny, drunkenness or, for having violated the Sabbath by working. Today, the totally restructured building is used for the major events in Lahaina.

*Lahaina: views of Front Street. This city that was capital of Hawai'i during the reign of Kamehameha II is now an important business and visitor center.*

*Left, Carthaginian II anchored in Lahaina harbor.*

As we go east on Front Street we will come to the **Holy Innocents Episcopal Church** that was established in 1862. The church is famous for its "Hawaiian Madonna", and the altar that is resplendent with the fruits, birds, fish and plants of Hawai'i. The entire old section of Lahaina is a National

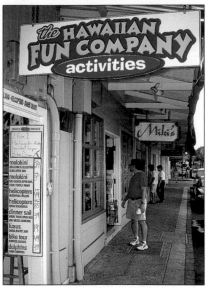

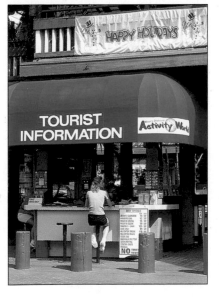

Lahaina's Front Street is the meeting place for local young people and constantly growing numbers of visitors. The street bustles with life and businesses, from shops selling flowery Aloha shirts to jewelry, from lively pubs to souvenir shops selling t-shirts and local crafts items.

The interior of the Lassen Gallery.

An unusual store insignia.

A gathering of gleaming Harleys.

Opposite page, unusual shots of daily life: a street preacher, a craftsman making a coconut frond hat, and a strolling photographer who lets visitors pose with his parrots – for that bit of local flavor.

Historical Landmark of the United States.

The stores along Front Street sell all types of goods, from precious jewels to souvenirs, from t-shirts to colorful, flower-printed *Aloha shirts*. There are many pubs and restaurants, ranging from the romantic and candle-lit to the **Hard Rock Café**, where there is no lack of lovely, well-tanned girls. Along with a tan, surfing and workouts, another must for young people who live on Maui and can afford it, is a Harley or a vintage American car from the 'fifties.

Lahaina – followed by Kīhei – is one of the island's main scuba diving centers – boats cast off daily from here for diving.

POSTCARDS MUST BE PICKED UP AT FOX PHOTO

# SUGAR CANE

As we travel around the island we will see extensive sugar plantations flanking the roads. To view them in all their splendor that is often augmented by the rainbows that appear after nearly every rainfall, we can take a ride on the **Lahaina Ka'anapali & Pacific Railroad**, commonly known as the *sugar-cane train*. The cars and steam engine are perfect replicas of the trains that operated in Hawai'i at the end of

the nineteenth century. The train provides scheduled service between Lahaina and the resort at Ka'anapali.

*A rainbow crowns the sugar cane fields.*
*Two shots of the "sugar cane train": the steam and engine and cars are faithful reproductions of late nineteenth century Hawaiian trains.*

*Opposite page, the West Maui Mountains seen from the Honoapiilani Highway.*

The West Maui Mountains are the vestiges of the island's oldest volcano. Centuries of erosion have created narrow valleys on the mountain slopes, while the area's high rainfall has led to the growth of lush vegetation.

# WEST MAUI MOUNTAINS

The island consists of two separate volcanoes that are connected by a strip of flat land where the town of Kahului is located. The most recent volcano, Haleakalā (10,023 feet/3060 meters) is the one that created the southeastern part of the island. Inside its enormous "crater" there are several cinder cones. The oldest volcano today is West Maui Mountains, the result of hundreds of years of erosion that transformed the volcano into a series of steep peaks separated by numerous deep, inaccessible valleys that gave the island its nickname of *The Valley Isle*. These splendid mountains are half as high as Haleakalā and are among the three wettest places on earth (about 390.3 inches/10 meters of rain a year).

The lava flows from the two volcanoes gave rise to plains characterized by very fertile soil, where most of the population and businesses have concentrated. In addition to the beautiful beaches, the northwestern coast of Maui is considered one of the most spectacular and colorful places anywhere: the red soil, the yellow-green of the cane fields and the

*Viewing the West Maui Mountains from above we can see the valleys that long and slow erosion has carved into the slopes of the volcano that are covered with lush plant life. Below, a spectacular view of Haleakalā's enormous crater, on the southeast side of the island. It was the eruptions of these two volcanoes that built the island of Maui.*

turquoise of the pineapple plants contrast brilliantly with the bright green of the West Maui Mountains that seem to be painted against the blue sky and white clouds that flutter around the peaks. The western coasts of Maui are protected from the winds and the waters are calm and clean – ideal conditions for snorkeling and scuba diving enthusiasts.

Whalers Village at Ka'anapali is a mall that also houses a museum dedicated to whales and whale-hunting that thrived throughout the nineteenth century.

Below: a whale skeleton on display at Whalers Village.

The northeast coast of Maui, between Kahana and Honokōwai offers striking vistas such as this.

# WHALERS VILLAGE

An interesting attraction at Ka'anapali is Whalers Village, a two-story outdoor mall which, in addition to restaurants and fashionable shops has a museum featuring historical items from the whaling period. There is shuttle bus service between the mall, the main hotels and the residential areas.

# PINEAPPLES

*Huge pineapple plantations create astonishing contrasts between the grey-green of the plants and the deep red colored earth.*

# KAPALUA

Kapalua Beach is located just a few miles north of Ka'anapali; it is home to the Kapalua Bay Hotel and the luxurious Ritz Carlton Hotel. The latter is surrounded by tennis courts and two beautiful, 18-hole golf courses where the greens are often crowned by rainbows that come out after every little rain shower. Nearby **Nāpili Bay** is a favorite destination for tourists, and a quiet, ideal place to rent an apartment far from the big visitor facilities. Nāpili and Kapalua offer some of the best beaches on Maui where you can swim or surf to your heart's content.

*A stretch of coast at Kapalua. The island's profuse vegetation thrives even on the black lava rock coast to the point that it seems to extend right into the water. The contours of the island of Moloka'i are visible in the background.*

On this and the following pages, views of Kapalua, one of the island's main resort towns, with luxurious hotels and enchanting beaches overlooking small bays.
Kapalua offers golf, tennis and riding, while all water sports, from swimming to sailboarding, from snorkeling to scuba diving are available in the coastal waters.

# GOLF COURSES

Golf is one of the most popular sports throughout the Hawaiian islands and that, of course, includes Maui, where several, large, avant-garde gold courses have been built in recent years. Hawai'i, today, is renowned among enthusiasts as one of the world's best golfing destinations. The archipelago has some of the world's most spectacular golf courses.

Many of the finest golf courses on Maui are located on the northern and southwestern parts of the inland, like Kapalua, Ka'anapali, Wailea and Makena. In general the courses feature 18 holes and are located within or near the hotel complexes that offer their guests the latest facilities to enjoy the sport in the greatest comfort and tranquility.

*Maui is truly a golfer's paradise: the island's courses are not only world renowned, they are backed by spectacular landscapes and scenery.*

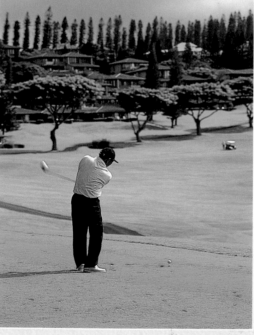

*On this page, some of the splendid golf courses at Ka'anapali and Kapalua that also feature championship courses.*

# HONOLUA BEACH

North of Kapalua the coast starts to get jagged, but the paved road goes as far as Honolua Bay which, together with Ho'okipa Beach Park (on the northwestern side of the island east of Kahului near Pā'ia) has made Maui the "Sailboarding Capital of the World", as we can see on many of the signs near the beaches.

Although Ho'okipa is very famous, the waves at Honolua are the real challenge. This is where the surfers feel themselves to be *in the Pope's living room* – the phrase used to describe the enormous tunnel waves…tunnels of water where the fearless – and sometimes reckless – glide on their boards at top speeds. The waters in these areas are only for the most skilled swimmers and surfers.

*Tunnel waves – the dream of all surfers, but reserved for the real experts – break on the jagged coast of Honolua Bay, north of Kapalua.*

# SURFING

*A surfer with a scooter searches the horizon waiting for the perfect waves.*
*Surfers at Ho'okipa Beach and Honolua Bay (in the large pictures) perform incredible stunts.*

A boat seems to sleep on a
truly "pacific" ocean while, in a
striking play of lights and
shadows, the setting sun paints
the sky and water in infinite
shades of yellow, red and
violet.

# MAUI OCEAN CENTER

As we proceed south from the northern coast we will come to the town of Ma'alaea that is home to the Maui Ocean Center, the new aquarium that was opened in March 1998. Its tanks host over 200 species of typical Hawaiian marine fauna. The most visited tank of all is the open ocean **Underwater Journey** that you can cross via a transparent acrylic tunnel and see the 18 grey reef sharks, an enormous spotted eagle ray, a pair of rays and a myriad of tropical fish. The tank holds nearly 8 hundred thousand gallons (3 million liters) of water.

The expert divers and marine biologists on the staff feed the Ocean Center's residents. Even the rays and eagle rays that live in the outdoor **Sting Ray Cove** tank get the same loving care.

*The Maui Ocean Center in the town of Ma'alaea was opened in 1998. It is home to over 200 species of Hawaiian marine animals. Top, spinner dolphins leap gracefully at the indoor tank at the Maui Ocean Center.*

*The transparent acrylic tunnel allows you to walk with the sharks, rays and other tropical marine life.*

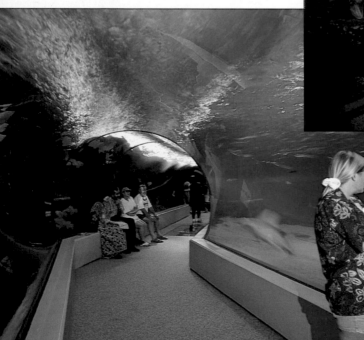

Thanks to the work of the Israeli engineer, Aharon Miroz, the Maui Ocean Center was one of the first aquaria in the world where a coral "rehabilitation" program was successfully tested. Damaged fragments of coral are removed from the sea and revived under optimum light, water and temperature conditions coupled with proper feeding that can be provided in the aquarium.

After "rehabilitation" the coral can be transplanted to the sea or used as artificial reefs in which other sea species can find a good home.

*The number and variety of specimens that live in the Maui Ocean Center tanks provide an excellent idea of the underwater world of the Hawaiian archipelago.*

*Above, a group of fascinated visitors watches a stingray being fed by a staff member.*

*Right, a grey reef shark seems to want to get a better look at those strange creatures who are watching him from the tunnel. Even though Hawai'i's waters are home to about 15 species of shark, the chances of actually meeting one are quite remote since few venture inside the reef, and those that do are much more interested in catching fish than swimmers!*

*Below, a group of visitors observing the animals in the Turtle Lagoon.*

# KĪHEI

Kīhei, that is located slightly south of Ma'alaea, is a modern town with many malls, bars, restaurants and beautiful beaches. This charming resort is the second town (in addition to Lahaina) from which diving boats sail for daily excursions that include two dives. As opposed to Lahaina, Kīhei does not have a sheltered harbor and perhaps it is the only place in the world where scuba operators are forced to slide into the water every day and recover their boats. This procedure, done with 4-wheel drive trucks complete with winches are simple even when dealing with boats longer than 30 feet (10 meters). With respect to Lahaina, Kīhei is the closest point (20 minutes by fast boat) to the Molokini Crater, the horseshoe-shaped islet that is considered one of the most beautiful diving spots on Maui. *To beat the wind*, as the local skippers say, you have to cast off at dawn so that you don't run into those strong waves that will be so helpful on the homeward trip.

About 7 miles south of Kīhei there is another important and luxurious resort, Grand Wailea Resort with two 18-hole golf courses, a large tennis court and five golden, arc-shaped beaches that are among the most beautiful in all the Hawaiian Islands. Nearby Makena Resort has five beautiful beaches, including one of the few with black sand on the island of Maui. We are now close to **Pu'u Ōla'i** a hill at the top of which the Pacific Whale Foundation operates an observatory where (from December through May) scientists and volunteers observe the migration of the humpback whales.

*Originally the stretch of coastline between Kīhei and Wailea, south of Ma'alaea was deserted and scattered with beautiful beaches.*
*Today, thanks to the modern irrigation systems, it is a string of modern condominiums, malls and big hotels which, along with the golf courses, tennis courts and other sports facilities fit into the landscape, enveloped by the greenery and colors of luxuriant plants.*

# LA PEROUSE BAY

Two more of Maui's famous beaches are located at the foot of the Pu'u Ōla'i hill: Big Beach and Little Beach. The latter is famous for the fact that it is a favorite spot for nudists. As we continue south, the asphalt is laid directly on top of solidified lava that flowed down the sides of the Haleakalā volcano when it erupted two hundred years ago. The road ends at La Perouse Bay, a protected nature and marine reserve, where black lava stone replaces the golden sands along the beach. The area that is subject to high, strong tides is not the ideal place for swimming.

*Views of the barren and inhospitable La Perouse Bay that opens south of Cape Kina'u at the foot of an impressive lava flow, from the last eruption of Haleakalā that occurred around 1790.*
*The bay gets its name from the French explorer, Jean François de Galaup, Count of La Perouse who landed here in 1786. Two years later he sailed for Australia and disappeared without a trace. Below, the volcanic rock marker with a memorial to the navigator set in the cove. Bottom, a close-up of a craggy block of solidified lava.*

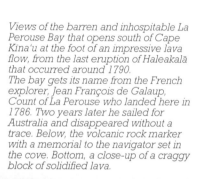

# MAUI TROPICAL PLANTATION

In the Valley Isle, in addition to the area's typical tropical vegetation, there are 700 other types of tropical and subtropical plants. To admire one of the most beautiful plantations on Maui we must head back towards Kahului and stop at the Maui Tropical Plantation near Waikapū. In addition to coffee, ginger, bananas and pineapples, the plantation grows colorful tropical flowers including one of Hawai'i's typical plants, the *bird of paradise*. The official flower of the Hawaiian Archipelago however, is the hibiscus that grows in a beautiful variety of colors: red, pink, yellow and orange.

*Three views of the Maui Tropical Plantation near Waikapū, on the strip of land that joins the West Maui Mountains to the majestic Haleakalā. Along with fruits – coffee, bananas, pineapple and ginger – the plantations also grow magnificent exotic flowers that add brilliant colors to the environment.*

# DOLPHINS

A thrilling and not-to-be missed experience is an encounter with wild dolphins. The Pacific Whale Foundation, a not-for-profit association that studies the behavior or these cetaceans, organizes one-day cruises to the nearby island of Lāna'i. As you near the island you may encounter groups of Spinner Dolphins. Frequently, the dolphins will swim near the boat and engage in acrobatic stunts that inevitably leave tourists speechless. The island of Lāna'i is also an excellent spot for scuba divers: the Lahaina Divers boats head out daily towards the lava rock grottoes and caverns along the coast. These grottoes are so huge that they are called cathedrals.

*Close encounters with spinner dolphins in the waters off the coast of Lāna'i.*

# HANDCRAFTS

Hawaiian crafts feature beautiful, finely carved wood figurines of local gods and goddesses as well as shell carvings and scrimshaw. Leis, the beautiful flower "necklaces" can be made of either real or artificial flowers. Other highlights of the local crafts include batik fabrics, colorful aloha shirts and flowery, surfer shorts.

*Tourists love the local, handcrafted wood and shell items.*

# FLOWERS

The island's geological color palette – red soil, dark lava rock, golden sands and black beaches – is complemented by the joyous hues of the plants. Trees, shrubs and plants in general seem to compete with each other to distinguish themselves, showing off their flowers and foliage in the greatest variety of shapes and shades.

The most common are orchids and hibiscus which, together with the plumeria, are the most frequently used blossoms in making leis.

*1. The Bird of Paradise, a south American plant of unusual shape and colors is related to the banana.*
*2. A variety of plumeria, an import from the tropical America.*
*3. The red ginger plant is also related to the banana.*
*4. Inflorescence of Pachystachys lutea: the white flowers stand out against the bright yellow of the bract.*
*5. The poinsettia is originally from Mexico.*

6.7.8. Three colorful hibiscus blossoms; the "native yellow" is Hawai'i's state flower.
9. The brilliant yellow of the flowering Cassia bush is striking against the green leaves.

10. The African Tulip Tree is a native of Africa: the flower petals are edged in yellow.
11. There are countless varieties of the Heliconia, another member of the banana family.

41

*Above and on the opposite page, pictures of the rain forest with the 'Iao Needle, a basalt rock formation, with the Kepaniwai Stream at its base.*

*Ka'ahumanu Church, with its graceful spire stands on High Street at Wailuku. The building dates from 1876 and is named for Queen Ka'ahumanu, the favorite wife of King Kamehameha I.*

# 'IAO VALLEY

If we take the road that leads from Waikapū to Wailuku, we will make a detour towards the 'Iao Valley, by taking a winding road that runs through the rain forest for a stretch of 8 miles (5 km). At the end of the road, we will proceed on foot for a short distance and come to the slopes of the **'Iao Needle**, a basalt rock formation with the **Kepaniwai Stream** running at its feet. The view is even more spectacular when seen from a helicopter. From the air we can see the tip of the needle and the waterfall on the eastern slope of the West Maui Mountains.

*On the opposite page, Kahakuloa Village, at the mouth of a valley that offers rich grazing land. Nestled in a protected bay south of a rocky promontory, the village is a place where time seems to have stopped and life moves along at a pace of days gone by.*

*Horses and cattle graze in the Upcountry breeding farms.*

## KAHAKULOA BAY

A nother truly spectacular stretch of coast starts at Kahului and traverses the typical and panoramic village of Kahakuloa that still shows us what the old Maui was.

## THE UPCOUNTRY

T he Upcountry, which is an inland part of the island, stands several hundred feet above sea level. Here the green meadows and hills are ideal grazing lands for cattle and horses. The landscape is so very different from the typical palm dotted beaches that it does not even seem like a tropical island.

# HO'OKIPA

Ho'okipa Beach Park is just a few miles northeast of Kahului along the Hāna Highway. This is where the world-famous surfing contest, the **Aloha Classic** is held every year. Thanks to the strong trade winds that blow from east to west 300 days a year creating the fantastic waves that break ceaseless on the beach, Ho'okipa has been nicknamed the wave machine.

But the ultimate in surfing waves is ''Jaws.'' A few miles north of Ho'okipa we find the world's biggest waves – and **National Geographic** dedicated an entire cover story to it. Jaws is an enormous semicircular wave: just when it is about to break, after having reached its maximum height it does indeed resemble the open jaws of a shark. To reach the big waves surfers are carried out by powerful jet-skis that leave them once they reach the top (about 50 feet/15 meters high). Some of the surfers say that the feeling they get as they ride in is like falling off a five-story building.

*A sign showing the turn-off for Ho'okipa along the Hāna Highway.*

*Ho'okipa Beach and Jaws are names famous among sailboarders and surfers around the world: here the waves reach heights of nearly 50 feet.*

# WINDSURFING

Colorful sailboards waiting to be rigged and taken out. Sailboarding on the frothy waves of Ho'okipa Bay.

*A detail of Hāna Bay, and, on the right, a local church.*
*Below, an African Tulip Tree in full bloom.*
*Opposite page, top: the black beach at Keʻanae. Bottom and on*
*the following pages, the spectacular views to enjoy along the*
*Hāna Road that some call Paradise Highway.*
*At every curve, this tortuously winding road opens onto*
*enchanting vistas that are probably the most beautiful in the*
*entire Pacific. As it winds through deep gorges crossed by*
*rushing streams, green fern-covered valleys, rough, steep walls*
*carved by waterfalls and projections of lava rock that are hit*
*endlessly by breaking waves, a drive along the Hāna Road is an*
*experience not to be missed.*

# HĀNA

The roughly 50 miles (84 kilometers) of roadway that link Kahului to the small town of Hāna can be covered in an amazingly short time. But, to cross the 54 bridges and 670 curves that make the Hāna Highway one of the curviest and spectacular panoramic roads in the entire Pacific requires a whole day. You cannot help but stop at the "scenic view areas" that offer an incredible vista of the ocean's blue striking the deep green of the rain forest and the spectacular waterfalls that crash down along lava rock walls. Along this road there are many side turnoffs that lead inland to villages where time seems to have stopped.

Paths crisscross tropical jungles streaked by waterfalls and where walnut, guava and pandanus trees grow. From the **Kaumahina State Park** look-out we can admire a stupendous view of the **Ke'anae** peninsula where there is a village surrounded by *taro* fields. The taro is the source of *poi* a thick paste that is the staff of Hawaiian food. It is interesting to note that there are over 30 different species of taro plants. When we are in the vicinity of the airport it means that we are just a short distance from **Wai'ānapanapa State Park** that offers a beautiful, black-sand beach. Once at Hāna, we can go over to **Red Beach**, the only red-sanded beach on the island. Here the atmosphere is tranquil and silent as opposed to the western shore. Charles Lindbergh (the aviator who made the first solo crossing of the Atlantic from the United States to Europe in 1927) was so fascinated by this spot that he decided to spend the final years of his life here.

Near the Hāna beach is the **Church of Wānanalua**, that was built by the first missionaries who came to Maui in 1838. Near the church there once stood the **Hotel Hāna-Maui** - the favorite spot of many international celebrities. Today the hotel is part of the ITT-Sheraton chain.

# 'ŌHE'O GULCH

Continuing on for a few more miles south of Hāna we will reach the 'Ōhe'o Gulch referred to as the Seven Pools, even though they are actually more than twenty-four. The pools are connected by cascades, where the water falls from one to the next to ultimately reach the ocean. If you like, you can stop and take a refreshing dip under one of the falls.

*Two views of the 'Ōhe'o Gulch, one of the most enchanting places along the Hāna Road.*
*The pools and waterfalls are fed by the 'Ōhe'o stream that begins on the slopes of Haleakalā.*

# HALEAKALĀ

We cannot leave Maui without taking a climb to its highest point, the crater of the world's largest active volcano, Haleakalā (10,023 feet/3060 meters) that has not erupted for over two centuries. The ideal is to arrive at Haleakalā ("House of the Sun" in Hawaiian) at dawn. After having driven through the deep blue night along a winding uphill road, we reach the Visitor Center. It is cold, and will be the first – if not the only time during your stay on the island that you will definitely need a sweater! Bring a flashlight and a tripod to take pictures of the dawn. The sun will come up slowly (keeping the promise it made to the demigod Māui) and the sky will gradually become red, pink, yellow and orange. It is an indescribable sight. In the distance, on a clear day you will see the peaks of the Mauna Kea and Mauna Loa volcanoes on the Big Island. As the light increases, the lunar landscape of the red-brown-grey volcano cones that appear from the enormous crater will become visible.

In the sunlight you can see how the flora changes from sea level to the peak of the volcano: it goes from tropical to rain forest to high forest to the aridity of a landscape of volcanic ash and rock. One of the few plants that do grow on the top of the volcano is silversword, a very rare plant. It flowers only once during its life and it grows on the Big Island's volcanoes too.

*The awesome "crater" of Haleakalā, "the House of the Sun"; in the box, the Visitor Center.*

*Two rare plants that live on this desolate land.*

If you have the time for the volcano excursion, you can go on a short hike, following one of the paths that goes into the crater. Maps are available at the Visitor Center.

The top of this volcano proved to the be ideal site for the construction of a complex of telescopes which, as we know, yield the best results when they are far from polluted skies and city lights. The observatory is near the Visitor Center, but it is not open to the public. It is a University of Hawai'i and Air Force research center.

*The lunar landscape that Haleakalā shows to those who venture into the enormous crater.*

*Opposite page, the sublime spectacle of dawn seen from the volcano and the observatory that stands out in stark white against the rocks.*

# THE UNDERWATER WORLD

The most famous diving point off the island of Maui is the crater of the extinct volcano, **Molokini**, an islet off the southwestern coast that offers the opportunity of choosing between a dive in currents on the external wall or the shallower waters inside that are also ideal for snorkeling. Along the outside wall of the crater (**Molokini Backside**) that goes down to a depth of over 390 feet (100 meters) you can encounter elegant manta rays, harmless grey reef sharks, eagle rays and graceful marine mammals like dolphins and humpback whales. All are easy to sight because visibility is excellent, often more than 100 feet (30 meters). The internal part of the crater (**Molokini Inside**) that slopes gently down to around 65 feet (20 meters) to disappear into the blue, is characterized by strips of sand that alternate with coral formations consisting of different species of hard corals that grow on a substratum of lava rock.

Oddly enough, there are no Gorgonia sea fans or soft corals in Hawai'i's waters. The waters inside the crater are famous for a myriad of unusual yellow butterfly fish and yellow striped snappers that surround and follow divers. Mike Severns, the famous underwater photographer and marine biologist who has been living on Maui for years wrote a book dedicated entirely to the species that populate the waters of Molokini. Mike and his wife, Pauline Fine Severns who is also a marine biologist, have discovered some of the species that are native to Hawai'i and they currently operate the Mike Severns Diving Center one of the many on the islands. Pauline often accompanies divers and helps them find rare and difficult to identify species, such as the beautiful frog fish, leaf fish, rare species of nudibranchiates and the funny looking rockmoover wrasse.
Dives along the western coast are limited by the lower visibility that is often not much more than 40 feet (10 meters), and the floor is flat and not more than

*Above, a green sea turtle photographed at Red Hill, and the shoals of Molokini Island. Below, a trigger fish, Hawai'i's state fish, in the waters of Black Rock; in the local language its name is Humuhumu-nukunuku-ā-pua'a.*

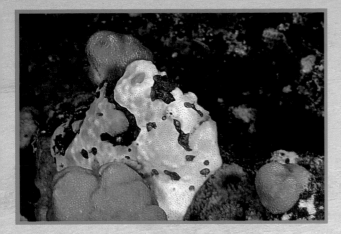

*Above and below, marine life in the waters near Molokini, a yellow frog fish and group of Raccoon Butterfly fish and Millet seed Butterfly fish. Right, a Moorish Idol at Wailea Point and a puffer fish at Black Rock.*

45-50 feet (15 meters) deep. Some places, like **Red Hill** south of Kīhei guarantee a very common encounter for Maui using just a mask, fins and snorkel: big green sea turtles (***Chelonia mydas***).
During their long stretches underwater they like to rest beneath the coral crags. The reef has many

*Above, a surgeon fish and left, a nudibranchs camouflaged on the ocean floor.*

*Center, an angel fish and a shark, above.*

*A diver meets a green sea turtle.*

"residents" including beautiful slate-grey sea urchins. The Hawaiian islands are also famous for the large variety of moray eels that populate the waters, but as opposed to those in other highly renowned diving spots, the Hawaiian varieties are less friendly, so be sure to keep your distance! The endemic species include the dragon moray that is easily recognizable because of the two horns on its head and its black and white spotted white-orange color. Another famous diving and snorkeling location south of Kīhei can be reached via the coast or by boat. It is known as **Five Caves** along the Makena coast where lava flows created a series of passageways, arches and grottoes inside of which there are often white tip reef shark. One of the easiest spots for diving or snorkeling from the shore, if we are on the northwestern part of the island is **Black Rock** north of Lahaina where just 40 feet (10 meters) of water offer a rich variety of marine fauna.

Thanks to its remote location, far from sources of pollution, the waters of the Hawaiian islands are extremely clear. Their isolation with respect to the other groups of islands led to the development of marine life with over 1000 different species that are nothing like anything we can see anywhere else in the world. That is why here in Hawai'i we can find more endemic marine species than in any other group of islands. Examples are the **Harlequin shrimp** and the **Picasso trigger fish** that is the state fish of Hawai'i, known in the local language as *Humuhumu-nukunuku-ā-pua'a*.

IMPORTANT WARNING: always remember that even when diving off the coast, the best time of day is morning, when the lack of wind makes for calm seas. Hawai'i is known for sudden changes in conditions where even a small increase in the waves creates strong currents beneath the surface and strong undertows that make going beyond the rocks very dangerous. Furthermore, the water temperature that ranges from 75 to 82° F (25 to 28°C) (slightly cooler than a tropical sea) makes it advisable to use an "under-suit" in addition to a normal, 3 mm diving suit. The best season for diving is from January to August.

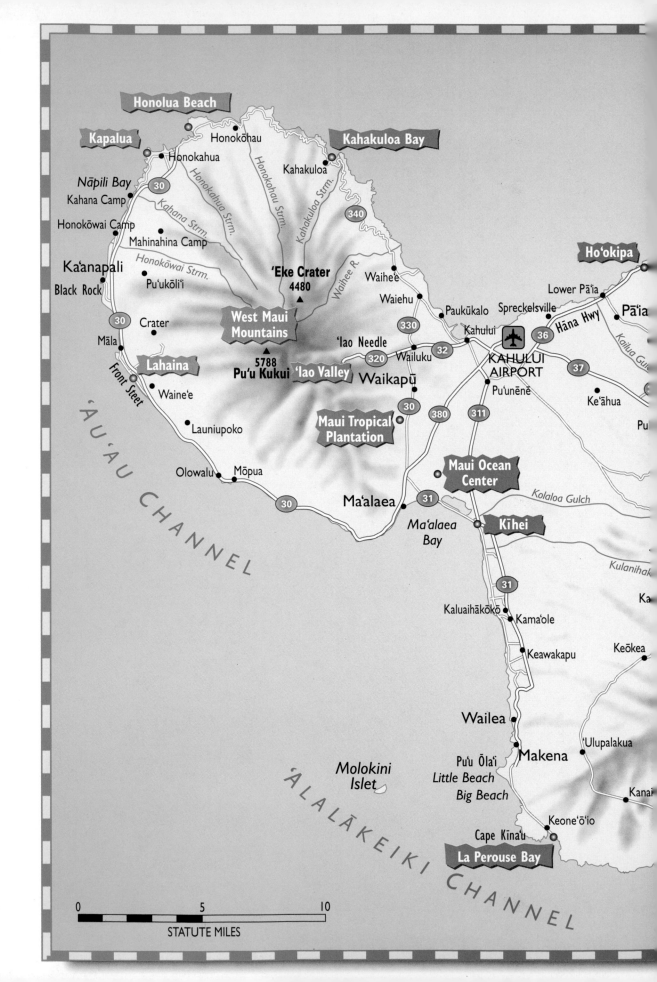

**Honolua Beach**

**Kapalua**

Honokōhau

**Kahakuloa Bay**

Honokahua

Kahakuloa

*Nāpili Bay*

Honokahua Strm.

Kahana Camp

Honokōhau Strm.

Kahana Strm.

340

Honokōwai Camp

Mahinahina Camp

**Ho'okipa**

Honokōwai Strm.

'Eke Crater
4480

Waihe'e

Lower Pā'ia

**Ka'anapali**

Waiehu

Spreckelsville

**Pā'ia**

Black Rock

Pu'ukōli'i

Paukūkalo

Kailua Gulch

Waihee R.

330

Kahului

Hāna Hwy

**West Maui
Mountains**

Crater

36

30

'Iao Needle

32

KAHULUI
AIRPORT

Ke'āhua

Māla

320

Wailuku

37

**Lahaina**

5788
Pu'u Kukui

'Iao Valley

Waikapū

Waine'e

Front Street

30

Pu'unēnē

Pu

Launiupoko

**Maui Tropical
Plantation**

30

380

311

Olowalu

Mōpua

**Maui Ocean
Center**

*Kolaloa Gulch*

'AU'AU CHANNEL

Ma'alaea

31

**Kīhei**

*Ma'alaea
Bay*

*Kulanihak*

31

Kaluaihākōkō

Kama'ole

Keōkea

Keawakapu

Ka

**Wailea**

*Molokini
Islet*

'Ulapalakua

Pu'u 'Ōla'i

**Makena**

*Little Beach*

*Big Beach*

Kana

Keone'ō'io

Cape Kīna'u

'ĀLALĀKEIKI CHANNEL

**La Perouse Bay**

0        5        10

STATUTE MILES

wela

Pe'ahi

Ulumalu

Huelo

Kaupakulua

Kokomo

Makawao

**Kaumahina
State Park**

**Ke'anae**

Wailua

Olinda

Nāhiku

Wai'ānapanapa
State Park

Honomā'ele

377

Ka'elekū

378

77

**Hāna**

**Hanakauhi**
8907

**Pōhaku Pālaha**
8105

9324

**Kalahaku
Overlook**

**Haleakalā Crater**

**Haleakalā
National Park**

Hāmoa

Waiohonu Strm.

10023

Visitor's
Center

Pu'uiki

**Red Hill**

Mu'ole'a

Hā'ō'ū

Koali

Pāhihi Gulch

Kipahulu

**'Ōhe'o Gulch
(Seven Pools)**

Mokulau

Kaupō

Nu'u

31

'ALENUIHĀHĀ CHANNEL

LOCATION:
north of the equator, in the middle of the Pacific Ocean. It is the second largest of the 8 big islands in the Hawaiian Archipelago.

POLITICAL STATUS
Hawai'i is the fiftieth state of the United States.
POPULATION STATISTICS:
Island of Maui: 117,644 (2000) - State of Hawai'i: 1,211,537 (2000)

CLIMATE:
tropical, mild and breezy all year.
Summer (May – September), warm and dry, with strong trade winds. Winter (October – April) cooler, and the trade winds are often affected by other weather events.

THE BEST TIME TO VISIT THE ISLAND:
from mid-May to the end of June, and from mid-September to late November.

LANGUAGE:
English is the official language, but some local people speak Hawaiian, a Polynesian language.

CURRENCY:
U.S. Dollar

TIME ZONE:
Greenwich Mean Time minus 11 hours.

TOURIST OFFICE:
Maui Visitors Bureau:
1929 Walipa Loop, Wailuku, tel 808 244 3530 – www.visit.Hawaii.org/

CONNECTIONS AMONG THE ISLANDS:
the islands are not far from each other and can be easily reached via small planes that offer daily flights. The airlines serving the area are: Aloha Airlines and Hawaiian Airlines.

HELICOPTER FLIGHTS

HAWAII HELICOPTERS:
Kahului Heliport – tel. 808 877 3900
toll free: 1 800 94 9099
website: www.hawaii-helicopters.com
e-mail: helitour@maui.net
The company offers 2 different itineraries to choose from. The most spectacular lasts 3 hours. The second itinerary is shorter, about 90 minutes. The helicopters have two engines, air conditioning and two pilots on board at all times.

ALEX AIR:
Kahului Heliport – tel 808 871 0792
toll free: 1 888 418 8458
website: www.mauigateway.com/alexair
e-mail: alexair@mauigateway.com
This company offers 10 itineraries to choose from. The helicopters are air conditioned.

WHALE WATCHING

PACIFIC WHALE FOUNDATION:
101 North Kīhei Road, Kīhei
tel 808 879 8811 / fax 808 879 2615
toll free: 1 800 942 5311
website: www.pacificwhale.org
e-mail: info@pacificwhale.org

THE STORE:
it is worthwhile stopping by to purchase a book, shirt or souvenir to remember your experience with whales and dolphins.
143 Dickenson Street, Lahaina.
The foundation has two boats that set out from Lahaina harbor 8 times a day, and two at Ma'alaea that make 7 trips daily. Each trip lasts about one hour and there is an expert who explains all about whales.
Whale sighting is guaranteed. If, for some reason you do not see a whale, the Foundation will let you sail out on the next trip – for free – until you see at least one!
The sighting experience is particularly thrilling when the whales jump out of the water (known as breaching) or when a hydrophone connected to amplifiers allows you to hear their songs. These cetaceans grow to nearly 50 feet in length, they love shallow waters and for this reason selected the 'Au'au channel between Maui and Lāna'i where the water is not more than 300 feet (100 meters) deep. The best time for meeting whales is from December to March (and February is considered the best of all!).
The Pacific Whale Foundation also studies the behavior of dolphins and organizes one-day cruises to the nearby island of Lāna'i where the boat is often surrounded by dozens of Spinner Dolphins engaged in waterbatics. The dolphin sighting excursions to Lāna'i last a full day and include: breakfast, barbecue lunch, coffee and fruit juice, a complete snorkeling lesson and equipment. During the outbound and inbound trips to Lāna'i, you may even see some whales!
During the outings the Pacific Whale Foundation gives its guests complete guides on the life of humpback whales and dolphins as well as a free poster.

DIVING CENTERS

MIKE SEVERNS
Kīhei, tel 808 879 6596
e-mail: severns@mauigateway.com
This center has an 11.5 meter boat that can carry up to 6 divers at a time, so that each gets excellent service. The boat makes daily outings to Molokini and the southwestern coast of Maui, departing from Kīhei. The biologist Pauline Fine Severns or her assistants are always on hand in the water to help divers identify the rare species of Hawaiian underwater life, and specifically the marine fauna off Molokini.

LAHAINA DIVERS:
143 Dickenson Street, Lahaina,
tel 808 667 7496
toll free: 1 800 998 3483
This is a 5 star PADI center that has two boats, one is 45 feet (14 meters) long and the other 55 (18 meters). They sail from Lahaina daily bound for Molokini, the southwestern coast of Maui where lava stone grottoes and caverns that are so big they are called the Cathedrals of Lāna'i.
All diving and snorkeling from the boats includes oxygen and leaded belts. The diving centers rent all the equipment you may need including cameras.

MAUI DIVE SHOP:
tel 808 879 3388
This is one of the biggest diving and snorkeling equipment retailers and rental outfits. There are eight Maui Dive Shops on the island. Its boats sail for Molokini, Lāna'i and turtle town on the coast for snorkeling and scuba diving.